Indian IT Industry: Problems and Applicable Labour Laws

By Siva Prasad Bose and Joy Bose

Contents

Dedication

This book is dedicated to all people employed by the IT industry and BPO industry in India.

Preface

The Indian IT industry has been a cornerstone of the country's economic growth, symbolizing innovation and global competitiveness. However, beneath its success lies a challenging reality for many employees. This book provides an in-depth exploration of the issues faced by IT professionals, including mass layoffs, health problems, and exploitative work conditions. It also sheds light on the labour laws applicable to the sector, including the significant reforms introduced by the Indian government through the labour codes of 2020.

Our goal is to not only highlight these challenges but also equip readers—whether they are IT employees, policymakers, or industry stakeholders—with the knowledge of their rights and the legal remedies available to them. By discussing real-world cases, historical contexts, and actionable strategies, we aim to foster greater awareness and inspire constructive changes within the industry.

We hope that this book serves as a resource for those navigating the complexities of employment in the IT sector and as a catalyst for improved working conditions and stronger legal protections. It is our belief that an informed workforce is an empowered one, capable of shaping a more equitable and sustainable future. The book is structured in two broad parts: the first half examines the problems and workplace realities faced by IT professionals through case studies and broader industry analysis, while the second half provides a detailed overview of the labour laws and legal codes applicable to the sector, along with practical guidance on remedies and worker organizing.

Acknowledgements

In writing this book, the authors gratefully acknowledge the following sources:

Labour and Industrial Laws Bare Act 2022, Commercial Law Publishers Pvt Ltd, 2022.

The Law Book: Big Ideas Simply Explained. By DK Publishing, 2020

Wikipedia https://www.wikipedia.org/

Ministry of Labour and Employment, Government of India https://labour.gov.in/

Chapter 1: Problems in the Indian IT Industry

In this chapter, we discuss the phenomenon of layoffs and other problems in the Indian IT Industry.

1.1 Scale of the Problem of Involuntary IT Layoffs

The Indian IT industry has been pivotal to the rise of India as the world's back office. According to NASSCOM, the Indian IT industry association, Indian IT companies commanded 55% of the $190 billion global IT and Business Process Outsourcing (BPO) market in 2017-18.

India's IT and BPO sector reportedly employed up to 5.4 million persons during the financial year 2023, generating around $245 billion in revenue, including $194 billion from exports. The IT services and BPO sectors contributed 7.4% of India's GDP in the financial year 2022.

Since the 1990s, the rapid growth of India's IT and BPO industries has been hailed by the Indian government as a means of accelerating economic development. Successive governments, at both state and national levels, have supported the IT and IT-enabled sectors with tax breaks, affordable land acquisition, and the establishment of Special Economic Zones (SEZs) with tax holidays and exemptions from standard labour and workplace laws.

However, outsourcing growth is slowing, and Indian IT companies lack the expertise to compete with major U.S. software firms like Google and Microsoft in developing software products. To maintain profitability, Indian IT companies have resorted to aggressive cost-cutting strategies.

Despite being a major source of foreign income, the Indian IT sector faces periodic waves of mass layoffs. These layoffs occur across multiple companies employing thousands of workers, especially in IT hubs like Bangalore, Noida, Hyderabad, and Gurgaon.

From 2014-2017, mass layoffs were prevalent in large IT companies like TCS, Infosys, and Wipro. This trend paused briefly during the COVID-19 pandemic but picked up again afterward. In 2019, for example, Capgemini reportedly laid off 5% of its Indian workforce—about 9,000 employees—while Tata Teleservices terminated around 500-600 employees. Although companies like Infosys denied mass firings, they acknowledged targeted layoffs for "low performers," hiring more fresh graduates to reduce costs.

Cognizant also implemented major layoffs in 2019, removing thousands of mid-level employees while shutting down its content moderation business, resulting in additional job losses. The layoffs aimed to save $500 million by 2021.

1.2 Factors behind involuntary IT Sector layoffs

Indian labour laws stipulate that companies must provide notice and severance pay during mass layoffs. However, many companies circumvent these laws by coercing employees into resigning, often under the pretext of poor performance.

Tools like the Bell Curve system are used to rank employees, designating a fixed percentage as "low performers," who are then terminated or placed on unproductive roles. This practice ensures cost reductions while skirting legal obligations.

The rise of automation and AI has also played a significant role in reducing jobs, with many managerial and decision-making roles now automated. Indian universities produce large numbers of IT graduates annually, many of whom lack employable skills, further saturating an already competitive job market.

Additionally, global factors such as economic slowdowns, the rise of cheaper IT labour markets in countries like Bangladesh and Vietnam, and anti-immigration policies in the U.S. have negatively impacted the Indian IT sector. For instance, a study by ASSOCHAM and KPMG reported that India loses approximately 70% of incremental voice and call center business to Asia and Eastern Europe.

1.3 Problems with working conditions of Indian IT employees

Though official working hours in the Indian IT sector are 8-9 hours per day, employees often work 10-12 hours or more due to project pressures. Many are also required to work weekends and holidays without overtime pay.

Health issues such as repetitive strain injuries (RSI), back problems, and stress-related illnesses are common. The intense work culture has also led to personal issues like marital conflicts, especially in households where both partners are IT professionals.

BPO workers face additional challenges, including erratic rotating shifts that disrupt sleep patterns and weaken immune systems. Female employees working late hours often face safety risks when commuting home.

1.4 Rise of IT Trade Unions

These mass firings have forced many Indian IT employees to form associations to safeguard their interests. This is despite the fact that Indian IT employees are paid typically higher salaries than other sectors and so often think of themselves as higher skilled professionals rather than as workers. This has given rise to a few IT unions around 2017-2020 and continuing.

Some such IT employee unions include the Karnataka IT/ITeS Union (KITU), based mainly in Bangalore, The Union of IT and ITES Employees (UNITE) trade union in Chennai and the Forum for IT Employees (FITE) also in Chennai. The major all India trade unions often offer support and affiliation to the IT unions, including the Centre of Indian Trade Unions (CITU) and the All India Trades Unions Congress (AITUC), INTUC etc.

Some of the employees affected by the layoffs, try to complain to the labour commissioners in their respective states, supported by such unions, or try the legal route to fight the firings, by citing existing laws such as Industrial disputes act that many companies do not follow.

There have been a few stories of success of IT employees against their sacking. In 2015, the firing of a female TCS employee was stayed by the Chennai high court citing her pregnancy and her allegation that she was being targeted unfairly because she was pregnant, forcing TCS to take back her termination. Another male TCS employee's termination was stayed by the same court citing the applicability of the industrial disputes act. But such victories are rare.

1.5 Conclusion

The Indian IT sector faces a paradoxical situation: it drives economic growth while grappling with systemic issues like job insecurity, unfair practices, and deteriorating working conditions. Addressing these challenges requires stronger legal enforcement and more robust worker protections.

While these systemic issues paint a daunting picture of the IT industry, it is essential to understand how these challenges translate to the individual level. The following chapter provides a case study of an IT professional, shedding light on the human cost of these industry-wide practices.

Chapter 2: Case study of an Indian IT Employee Who is Asked to Resign

In this chapter, we provide a case study of an IT professional who faced pressure to resign from their company. While the scenario described may be hypothetical, it reflects the common experiences of many IT employees in India.

2.1 Background

S (name changed) worked for a well-known multinational company. A few months prior, the company announced that its profits had decreased compared to previous years due to increased competition. In response, the management decided to identify and remove so-called low-performing employees during the annual appraisal process.

The company used a bell curve ranking system to assess performance, where a fixed percentage of employees were classified as low performers relative to their peers. This time, the percentage of employees receiving low ratings was significantly increased to align with the cost-cutting strategy. Unfortunately, S was one of the employees labeled as a low performer.

2.2 The Resignation Pressure

One day, S's manager had a private conversation with him, informing him that his performance was deemed unsatisfactory and advising him to begin searching for another job. The manager explained that S would need to leave the company within two months.

Shortly afterward, the Human Resources (HR) department also contacted S, echoing the same message. S protested, asserting that his performance was adequate and providing evidence of his contributions. Despite his appeals to higher management, no action was taken to reverse the decision.

HR pressured S to resign voluntarily, threatening that a formal termination would include negative remarks in his exit documents, potentially affecting future job prospects. Many of S's colleagues, facing similar pressure, chose to resign.

2.3 S's Response and Outcome

After careful consideration, S decided not to resign. Instead, he avoided calls from HR, communicated exclusively through email to document all interactions, and repeatedly requested more time to find a suitable job.

HR continued to exert pressure, but S remained firm, knowing that forced resignation is not legally valid. Over time, the company faced an unexpected wave of attrition as even high-performing employees began resigning due to the toxic work environment. This increased turnover caused project delays and created operational challenges for the company.

Eventually, due to improved quarterly performance and the growing attrition problem, HR stopped pressuring employees like S to resign. S continued to work at the company and remains employed there to this day.

2.4 Conclusion

This case study highlights the pressures faced by Indian IT employees during layoffs or cost-cutting measures. S's experience underscores the importance of understanding one's rights and resisting undue pressure to resign. By standing firm and documenting interactions, employees can protect themselves from unfair practices and navigate challenging situations more effectively.

S's experience is not an isolated incident but part of a growing trend in the IT industry. Contract labour, often seen as a cost-cutting measure, further exacerbates job insecurity, as explored in the next chapter.

Chapter 3: Contract Labour in the Indian IT Industry

In this chapter, we discuss the growing trend of contract labour in the Indian IT industry, its implications for workers, and the relevant legal framework governing such practices.

3.1 Rise of Contract Labour in IT

The use of contract labour has seen a significant rise in the Indian IT industry. Contract labour consists of individuals who are not permanent employees of the companies for which they work. Instead, they are hired and remunerated by third-party contractors.

This trend has grown globally, with an increasing number of flexible and temporary job roles. Reports indicate that as much as 30% of the workforce in major Indian IT firms consists of contract labourers. Companies use contract labour to save costs and reduce statutory obligations, such as benefits and protections under labour laws.

In the U.S., similar trends exist, with estimates suggesting that up to 30% of American workers hold temporary or low-wage jobs. Studies predict that nearly half of all new jobs in the post-recession U.S. could be temporary.

3.2 Characteristics and Challenges of Contract Labour

Contract work is marked by several drawbacks for employees:

- Inferior employment status compared to regular employees.

- Lack of job security and easier termination procedures.

- Limited or no access to benefits like health insurance, paid leave, or retirement pensions.

- Lower salaries, often significantly less than those of permanent employees performing similar work.

The ambiguous responsibility between the contracting company and the hiring company creates further vulnerabilities, leaving workers uncertain about who is accountable for their rights and benefits.

3.3 Legal Framework Governing Contract Labour

In India, the Contract Labour (Regulation and Abolition) Act, 1970, governs the employment of contract labour. The Act applies to establishments employing 20 or more workers and mandates:

- Registration of the principal employer (the company where work is done).

- Licensing of contractors.

- Provisions for workers' wages, amenities, and other conditions.

The law prohibits the use of contract labour for work of a perennial nature or work necessary for the establishment's core operations. Workers performing the same type of work as regular employees are entitled to equal pay and benefits.

However, in practice, many provisions of the Act are ignored or poorly enforced. For example, contract labourers are often paid significantly less for performing the same tasks as regular employees, violating the law.

3.4 Implications for the IT Industry

If the Contract Labour Act were strictly enforced, it would be illegal for companies to employ contract workers on long-term IT projects without offering them the same wages and benefits as regular employees. This could disrupt cost-saving measures commonly practiced by IT firms.

Despite the IT sector generating around 100,000 new jobs annually, it struggles to accommodate the approximately 200,000 engineering graduates entering the job market. This oversupply of job seekers fuels the growth of contract labour and exploitation, as many are willing to accept subpar working conditions.

3.5 Conclusion

The rise of contract labour in the Indian IT industry reflects a global trend toward cost-cutting and workforce flexibility. While legal frameworks exist to protect contract workers, weak enforcement often leaves them vulnerable to exploitation. Greater awareness of labour rights and stricter implementation of existing laws are essential to ensuring fair treatment of contract workers in the IT sector.

The prevalence of contract labor reflects broader transformations in the tech industry, a theme extensively explored in books that delve into the culture and challenges of the IT sector. The next chapter reviews such works to provide additional perspectives.

Chapter 4: Books About Working in the Tech Industry and IT Sector

In this chapter, we review a selection of books that critically explore the experiences of working in the tech industry and IT sector. Although most of these books are focused on the Silicon Valley culture in the U.S., they also provide valuable insights applicable to India's IT industry, as many Indian IT professionals work for global companies or under similar conditions.

4.1 Lab Rats: why modern work makes people miserable, by Dan Lyons

The highly readable book by Dan Lyons goes into the nature and pace of work that is normal and expected in the tech industry today and tries to analyze why it makes people want to escape from it.

Lyons starts with some examples of how employees are often forced or 'encouraged' to take team workshops (example: Lego workshops) that claim to improve work productivity but in fact encourage conformity, a shared psychosis and group delusion (thinking the products would somehow change the world) in the name of cultural fit. He also surveys what is wrong with imposing methodologies such as Agile, Holacracy or Lean startup, with lots of new terminologies and processes but little value add.

Lyons further describes some common factors in the way the industry works that contribute to worker unhappiness, stress, low job satisfaction and health issues. These include the constant feeling of job insecurity or fear of being fired, the lowering of salaries (in absolute terms) than a generation ago, exposure to constant change at small and big levels (such as frequent reorgs) that leads to weariness, and finally the constant surveillance and monitoring of employees, enhanced with AI and related technologies, that leads to dehumanization. He mentions how the fear of losing large unvested stock options, if they are fired before the vesting time, keeps employees constantly on their toes and willing to overwork.

Finally, Lyons shows how many tech startups are fueled by a ruthless dog eat dog venture capital scenario, and reviews some Silicon Valley companies that are going against all these tendencies and seem to genuinely care for employees.

4.2 Live work work work die by Corey Pein

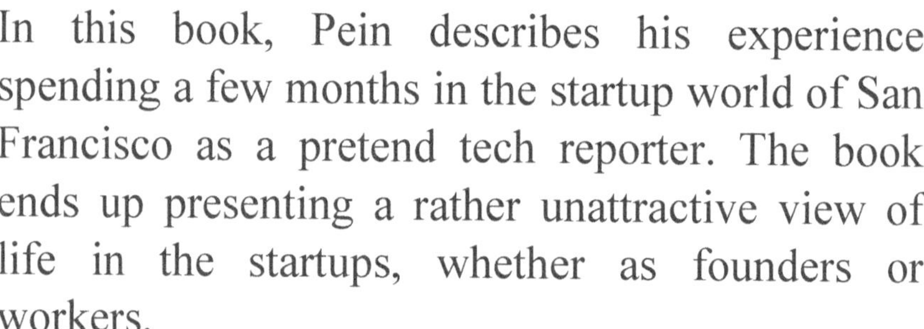

In this book, Pein describes his experience spending a few months in the startup world of San Francisco as a pretend tech reporter. The book ends up presenting a rather unattractive view of life in the startups, whether as founders or workers.

He describes how tech wannabe people are forced, thanks to astronomical rents, to live in cramped living spaces shared with many others. On the other hand, old timers in rented houses are forced out by greedy landlords eager to take advantage of the tech bubble.

Pein further reveals some of the murky goings-on in a few startups. He surveys how the gig economy of tech works, fueled by startups such as Fiverr. He then goes on to some history of the Silicon Valley, how it all began and the humble origins and unsavory actions of some tech giants such as Uber.

Pein finally describes his experience of pitching a tongue in cheek startup idea for Y combinator, a system that funds and incubates selected startups which survive the tough competition and successfully pitch their idea. He also discusses the crazy views of a few startup founders that seem to condone things like racism, authoritarianism, and cyborg evangelism.

4.3 The burnout society and Psychopolitics: neoliberalism and new technologies of power by Byung Chul Han

These books, burnout society and psychopolitics, are written by a philosopher and probably belong more to a philosophy article. The reason I include them here is that they throw some light on the psychology of working in modern tech companies, how employees are encouraged by modern management practices, to internalize the control mechanism and demands of their work, no matter how unreasonable. Similar techniques as are used to increase consumption of manufactured products are also used to increase the productivity of employees in tech companies.

In the book Burnout Society, Byung Chul Han discusses how our modern society has become an achievement based society rather than a discipline based society as in the past centuries. In such a society, instead of employers having to discipline employees to work harder by using force, modern management theory gives employees the freedom to work as hard, or not, as they wish. However this very freedom ends up as a paradox, thanks to the primacy given in this society to achievement. The employees feel they have to achieve more to get higher status and so force themselves to work harder than they otherwise would. This situation, on the other hand, leads to an excessiveness of positivity (what he terms brain doping) and ends in exhaustion and depression culminating in burnout.

In Psychopolitics, Byung Chul Han first focuses on the all pervading surveillance and lack of privacy of consumers (and employees), thanks to big data and sophisticated tools. He finds the situation similar to a panopticon, a jail where all prisoners are monitored round the clock. Han then goes on to how the system of modern capitalism manipulates emotions (such as encouraging a constant feeling of anxiety) to increase consumption and uses sophisticated tools such as gamification to increase productivity. For employees, the same method of constant anxiety (threat of losing jobs for example) would be used to motivate them to increase the work productivity. So instead of having to have surveillance, this method is more powerful in that employees can internalize the values and work harder. He finally discusses how the ubiquity of big data or what he calls dataism takes away the pretence of free choice of the consumers.

4.4 A people's history of Silicon Valley by Keith Spencer

This book sees the Silicon Valley tech industry as a whole rather than just focus on lives of tech employees. It goes into the geography and history of the Silicon Valley, how it used to have various industries in previous generations and tech industry is merely the latest industry to call it home. It discusses how the tech industry is truly global: while the iphone may be designed in California the parts are assembled in China and the raw materials like Cobalt come from Congo in Africa. And in these places too such as China and Africa, workers producing parts for the tech industry are heavily exploited. The wealth of the tech billionaires is built on the labour of these people too. So we should not look at Silicon Valley in isolation.

The book then reviews the history of the Silicon Valley. First were the Ohlone people who lived simple lives that were in harmony with nature, before the coming of the Spanish. The Spanish and the later American settlers killed a large number of Ohlone. Then California became a part of Mexico before joining the United States. The area was home to a thriving fruit industry that produced oranges, also other industries like wines developed here. After World War II, the US government poured billions of dollars of defense money into the institutions and companies here via NASA and DARPA. Stanford University, for example, benefited from this government funding of research projects and gave rise to a number of tech startups, both hardware and software related, in the bay area.

After this, the book discusses the counterculture of the 1960s which gave rise to the tech hippies, people like Steve Jobs, who had visions of changing the world. The trend of designing tech offices with their bright colors and play areas and free coke comes from this idea that tech are somehow not like other industries, and is going to make the world a better place with their innovative products. These kinds of beliefs make the tech industry and its companies similar to cults in a way. Included in such beliefs is that the tech employees are special and there is no classism or racism in the industry, it is somehow above all this. Another common belief is a rosy view of the future, that somehow tech can solve all of humanity's problems.

The book also goes into the transformation of the Silicon Valley from its days where misfits and geeks were at home, where hobby clubs like Homebrew designed the first personal computers, to the modern days where it is now very much a part of the mainstream culture. It describes the early Microsoft — IBM — Apple wars and their contrast with the GNU free software movement. It also goes into labour practices of the software companies, such as how the big tech companies collude to keep salaries low, how the Bay area locals got displaced by the technocrats due to rising rents, how women engineers were discriminated due to pay differentials and the machismo culture.

The book then discusses the origins of the web from ARPANET days to the dot com bubble which burst and many companies became bankrupt, to the rise of social media, especially Facebook. It mentions how Facebook tries to keep its users addicted to the platform using psychological tools, causing things like loneliness and depression in many users, sells consumer data to advertisers, how Facebook ads are sometimes used by powerful entities to spread disinformation and how it is leading to a decline in journalism as news companies are laying off reporters and going bust. It then speaks of the rise of the mobile phone and how apps like Uber have given rise to the gig economy. It calls the phenomenon of companies providing renting services rather than products as the rentier economy. Finally, it goes into companies like Google helping form a type of surveillance state and the dangers to democracy by the ubiquity of tech.

4.5 The attention merchants: the epic struggle to get inside our heads by Tim Wu

Tim Wu explores how companies like Google and Facebook monetize user attention through targeted advertising. He warns of the societal consequences of this attention economy, including addiction, privacy violations, and the commodification of human focus.

4.6 World without mind by Franklin Foer

World Without Mind

**WHY GOOGLE, AMAZON,
FACEBOOK AND APPLE
THREATEN OUR FUTURE**

Franklin Foer

In this book, Foer focuses on the big four tech companies and their practices. These big 4 hold a near monopoly in their respective domains: Google (knowledge), Facebook (social media), Amazon (commerce) and Apple (premium gadgets especially mobile phones). He discusses how monopoly in each area, free from regulatory controls and constraints, is the only logical end for Silicon Valley companies. Then he goes through each of the big companies in turn and discusses their aims and strategies to dominate the market, how they act as gatekeepers and controller of knowledge, issues related to political activism and assault on journalism and democracy by these companies, and other downsides of the dominance of each of these monopolies on the wider society. Overall they lead to a world without mind, where users, suppliers, consumers, and entire industries have to comply with the new norms established by these companies in order to survive. Finally, he discusses how to fight back against such monopolies and usher in a world where free thinking, creativity, data privacy and free choice can once again become the norm.

4.7 The People vs Tech by Jamie Bartlett

This book focuses on the impact of tech on politics and democracy. It discusses issues such as the erosion of free will thanks to targeted personalized ads (thanks to large scale collection of user data by the big tech companies, combined with market research and behaviorist theories) telling us what to watch, what to like and what to buy. It also discusses the tribalisation of politics thanks to social media companies, resulting in polarization and clustering of users into digital 'tribes', of people belonging to both left and right wing of politics, based on group identity rather than logic. It also discusses issues such as the erosion in capacity of citizens to make judgments on what is good for them due to the increased use of AI assistants, interference of tech on free elections (reference to the Cambridge Analytica scandal), increased inequality and gentrification of cities, monopolistic tendencies of the big tech companies, lack of accountability and so on. Finally, it discusses crypto anarchy and rise of technologies such as bitcoin, as a kind of backlash against increased centralization and authoritarianism.

4.8 Disrupted: Ludicrous misadventures in the tech start up bubble by Dan Lyons

In this humorous account, Dan Lyons shares his experience working in a tech startup. He reveals the absurdities of startup culture, including exploitative management practices, unrealistic expectations, and a toxic work environment.

4.9 Chaos monkeys: inside the Silicon Valley money machine by Antonio Garcia Martinez

García Martínez provides an insider's view of Silicon Valley, describing the chaotic and cutthroat nature of startups and their eventual acquisitions by big tech firms. The book offers a brutally honest look at the highs and lows of startup life.

4.10 The TCS Story and Beyond by S.Ramadorai

This book is written by the founder of Tata Consultancy Services or TCS, S Ramdorai. TCS is the company with one of the biggest turnovers in the Indian IT industry and one employing the largest number of IT workers. In this book, the author speaks about the history of TCS and the struggles it had to go through since its earliest days since its founding in 1968, how it built up its workforce and how it obtained projects from abroad. It also speaks a little bit about how its corporate culture evolved and what makes the company tick.

4.11 Conclusion

The books discussed in this chapter provide valuable perspectives on the tech industry, from its culture and labour practices to its societal impacts. They offer both cautionary tales and critical insights, helping readers better understand the challenges faced by tech workers and the broader implications of the industry's growth.

The issues highlighted in these books underscore the critical role of labour laws in addressing inequities and protecting workers' rights. The next chapter provides an overview of the legal framework that governs labour in India.

Chapter 5: Introduction to Labour Laws in India

In this chapter, we introduce the concept of labour laws and provide an overview of their evolution in India, as well as some international labour standards. This is relevant to the IT sector, just like all other service sectors where labour is abundantly used.

5.1 What are Labour Laws

Labour laws govern the relationship between employers and employees, setting the conditions for employment, work practices, industrial disputes, strikes, and union activities. These laws also cover termination, retrenchment, and protections for employees against unfair treatment or dismissal. For example, if an employee is fired unfairly, they can seek recourse through labour laws by filing a complaint with the labour commissioner or pursuing legal remedies. Similarly, labour laws regulate the formation and functioning of unions, ensuring fair practices for collective bargaining and dispute resolution.

5.2 Evolution of Labour Laws in India

Labour laws in India have their origins during British colonial rule and have evolved significantly since independence.

Under British Rule

The industrialization of India under British rule led to the emergence of a labour force and the establishment of early labour laws. Key laws enacted during this time include:

- Indian Slavery Act, 1843

- Workmen's Compensation Act, 1923

- Indian Trade Unions Act, 1926

- Payment of Wages Act, 1936

- Industrial Employment Standing Orders Act, 1946

Labour strikes were common during this period, demonstrating the growing strength of organized labour. Examples include the 1921 Buckingham and Carnatic Mills Strike and the 1928 South Indian Railway Strike.

After India became independent, a number of protections for labour were included in the constitution of India.

Post-Independence Era

After gaining independence, India included labour protections in its Constitution. New laws were introduced to safeguard workers' rights, such as:

- Industrial Disputes Act, 1947

- Minimum Wages Act, 1948

- Factories Act, 1948

Recent Developments

In 2020, the Indian government consolidated multiple labour laws into four comprehensive codes to simplify and modernize the legal framework:

1. Code on Wages, 2019

2. Industrial Relations Code, 2020

3. Occupational Safety, Health and Working Conditions Code, 2020

4. Code on Social Security, 2020

5.3 International Labour Organization ILO

ILO is one of the constituents of the United Nations or UN, which is the main international body consisting of representatives of all the nations. ILO was founded in 1919 under what was then the League of Nations, precursor to the United Nations. It is responsible for formulating a set of labour standards to which all the countries in the world are aimed to align their labour laws.

It was responsible for the Declaration on Fundamental Principles and Rights at Work, which was adopted in 1998 and included sections on collective bargaining, forced labour, child labour and discrimination. The core conventions include the right to form unions and collective bargaining, industrial action or strikes, abolition of forced labour and child labour, and removal of all forms of discrimination at work.

Other conventions of the ILO include provisions for maternity leave and maternity protection at work.

5.4 Main Labour Laws in India

The main labour laws in India include the following:

- Industrial Disputes Act 1947

- State Shops and Establishments Act

- Workmen's Compensation Act 1923

- Trade Unions Act 1926

- Industrial employment standing orders act 1946

- Payment of wages act 1936

In India there are 204-210 labour laws, out of which around 44 apply on a day-to-day basis. This was before the simplification of the laws in 2020.

The new labour codes introduced in 2020 aim to simplify and consolidate these laws for better enforcement and compliance.

5.5 Practical implications of labour laws

Some of the general characteristics of employment and other practical implications of important Indian labour laws are as follows:

The service conditions for employees have to be defined: This is as per the Industrial Employment Standing Orders Act. This is needed so that the employees can know what are the conditions of employment they are working with. These include things like working hours, paid leave, gratuity and so on. These are called standing orders. The standing orders act is applicable for 50+ employees in an establishment. The deputy labour commissioner is the certified authority for the purpose of ensuring this.

The standing orders give information including name of company, working hours, service condition, on what terms appointed/separated, how one must terminate employees, how workers get exit, misconduct and so on. There is a model standing order, which is to ensure that the companies cannot go beyond that model. If the standing order for a specific firm or establishment incorporates illegal terms, such as stating a bond or restricting the ex-employee from joining a competitor, they can be challenged.

However, in certain sectors and states, such as for the IT industry in Karnataka state, the government can pass an exemption for whole of the industry, saying standing orders act is not applicable to IT industry.

Definition of employee and management: This comes under the industrial employment standing orders act. As per the act, a supervisor or manager is one who has administrative powers, e.g. granting leave, reports, granting permissions etc, discharged on a continuous basis. If one occasionally has to discharge such powers during course of work, then he would be classified as a workman and not as a supervisor. It should be noted that standing orders act is only applicable to establishments having 50 or more employees.

Grievance mechanism: A grievance mechanism or procedure for redressal is required to be set in every establishment. The labour commissioner is the appellate authority for violations. There is a clause in standing order, not in letter and spirit, which is permission to prosecute. If such a mechanism is not present (apart from the sexual harassment mechanism which is also needed) it can be challenged.

Laws related to dispute related to termination or retrenchment: This comes under the Section 2(K) of Industrial disputes act. In case of termination or retrenchment, any individual can lay an industrial dispute. An industrial dispute is a dispute between an employee and a company. For things like denial of promotion etc, it can a collective dispute between the employees and the management of the firm, and therefore the employees need a union to fight for their behalf. A union need not be connected to a particular establishment or a particular industry. If there is presently no union for a specific industry or establishment, any general union such as CITU or AITUC or INTUC or Bharatiya Mazdoor Sangh can also support the petition of the worker.

The procedure in case of industrial disputes is as follows: the employees or the trade union approach the labour committee set up within the company, who first try to explore reconciliation between the employees and management via discussion. If the reconciliation is not fruitful, then the case goes to the labour commissioner, who gives his verdict and sends to government which sends it to the court whose jurisdiction falls in that area.

Often, employees do not approach courts fearing blacklisting from jobs in the future, however such blacklisting is also against the law. Every employee has a right to equality (article 14) and livelihood (article 21) - these are fundamental rights granted to all citizens by the

Indian constitution. Article 19 of the constitution is the right to form associations.

Law in Special economic zones or SEZs: After liberalization, the government of India has set up many Special Economic Zones or SEZs, mainly to attract foreign investment. In SEZs also the labour laws are applicable. The main difference is that there may be specific exemptions, also the company needs to be informed in advance if the labour commissioner or other labour authorities come for an inspection of the premises at a specific pre-arranged time.

Forceful resignation: This comes under the Industrial Disputes act, under the section related to unfair labour practices, including acts of force or violence. Nobody can force the employee to resign. There are 5 schedules in Industrial Disputes act, which industries, which jurisdiction, which are conditions of service, which notices etc. These are applicable to every factory, establishment, individual. Even one employee.

Changes to terms and conditions of work: If the management of the establishment wish to change the mode of payment of wages, or some other condition of work such as PF, extend shift timings etc, they have to give the employee a 21 days notice. The employees can challenge the notice before the labour department, and the execution of the change is automatically stayed if such a challenge is made. Shift working and related matters come in the 4th schedule of the Industrial disputes act.

Unfair labour practices: If the employers interfere, refrain, or coerce the employees against joining or assisting a trade union, or threaten the employees with discharge or dismissal for trade union activities, the employees can file a complaint before the labour secretary of the state government.

Similarly, if the management forms a counter trade union, that is also an unfair labour practice. Similarly, discharging an employee for participating in a strike called by a trade union, also not allowed.

Layoff procedure: This is related to the Industrial Disputes Act section 2K. If more than 100 workmen are employed by the establishment, then prior permission must be taken before laying them off. If the number of employees is greater than 50 and less than 100, then 2 months of notice must be given. If it is less than 50 then full 100% wages has to be paid during the period of layoff.

Inspectors have to check whether the law of the land has been followed or not. In case of company closure, retrenchment, or layoff in an establishment of greater than 100 employees, the company has to apply to the secretary of labour department of the government for permission. If they take any other mode, the court will go deeper into the matter. If the labour commissioner files a complaint, the labour secretary will give relief to the employees. If employees are organized in a trade union, they can force the court to act. But many times, employees are weak and do not want to take risks. If company says stoppage of production (to justify termination of employees), but whole company is not closed and no wages are given, that too is illegal. These problems can only be solved collectively, not individually, by means of trade unions. Thus, trade unions perform an invaluable service of protection and support of the employees.

5.6 Conclusion

Labour laws in India have evolved to balance the interests of employers and employees, providing essential protections for workers. The recent consolidation into four labour codes marks a step toward streamlining these laws, but effective enforcement remains key to their success.

Understanding the evolution and scope of labour laws is essential to appreciating their application. The next chapter delves into the Industrial Employment Standing Orders Act, a cornerstone of workplace regulations in India.

Chapter 6: Industrial Employment Standing Orders Act

In this chapter, we discuss the Industrial Employment Standing Orders Act, 1946, which mandates employers to establish clear terms and conditions of employment to ensure transparency and fairness in the workplace.

6.1 Introduction to the standing orders act

Before the enactment of the Standing Orders Act, workers in Indian establishments often faced arbitrary and inconsistent employment rules. Employers could change policies unilaterally, leaving employees vulnerable to exploitation.

The Act was introduced to standardize employment practices and make them transparent. It applies to all industrial establishments employing 100 or more workers, though exemptions exist for certain sectors and states as per government notifications.

Figure: First Page of the Standing Orders Act 1946

6.2 What are standing orders

Standing orders define the rules and conditions of employment in an establishment. These include:

- **Classification of Workers**: Categorization as permanent, temporary, apprentice, etc.

- **Work Details**: Processes for communicating work responsibilities and salary structures.

- **Attendance and Leave**: Policies for attendance, late arrivals, shift timings, and leave applications.

- **Entry and Search Rules**: Regulations for entering the premises and permissible searches.

- **Disciplinary Actions**: Guidelines for termination, suspension, and misconduct handling.

- **Redressal Mechanisms**: Processes for employees to seek remedies against unfair treatment.

6.3 Certification and posting of standing orders

The standing orders act holds that the standing orders for any establishment need to be certifiable, as long as they are in conformity with the standing orders act. Workers or trade unions can raise objections to any of the conditions, and the certifying officer can adjudicate on the fairness or reasonableness of any of the standing orders. Their judgments shall be binding on the parties, however they can be appealed at an appellate authority. The certification and appellate authorities have the power of a civil court.

Once they are certified, the standing orders shall be posted in the establishment in English on special notice boards near the entrance where they can be visible to all the workers.

The Act also addresses situations where workers are suspended pending investigation. In such cases:

- For the first 90 days, suspended workers are entitled to 50% of their wages.

- For the remaining period, they are entitled to 75% of wages unless the delay is caused by the worker.

6.4 State-Specific Amendments

While the Act applies across India, states like Karnataka and Maharashtra have introduced specific amendments. For example, IT industries in some states are exempt from the Act under government notifications, often citing the unique nature of the sector.

6.5 Conclusion

The Industrial Employment Standing Orders Act ensures clarity and fairness in employment practices by requiring employers to define and display work conditions. While the Act has improved workplace transparency, exemptions in certain sectors highlight the need for balanced implementation to protect workers' rights.

Chapter 7: Trade Unions Act

In this chapter, we discuss the Trade Unions Act, 1926, which regulates the establishment, registration, rights, and functioning of trade unions in India. This Act has been instrumental in fostering collective bargaining and protecting workers' rights.

THE TRADE UNIONS ACT, 1926

ACT NO. 16 OF 1926[1]

[*25th March*, 1926.]

An Act to provide for the registration of Trade Unions and in certain respects to define the law relating to registered Trade Unions [2]***.

WHEREAS it is expedient to provide for the registration of Trade Unions and in certain respects to define the law relating to registered Trade Unions [2]***; It is hereby enacted as follows:—

CHAPTER I

PRELIMINARY

1. Short title, extent and commencement.—(*1*) This Act may be called the [3]*** Trade Unions Act, 1926.

[4][(*2*) It extends to the whole of India [5]***.]

(*3*) It shall come into force on such date[6] as the Central Government may, by notification in the Official Gazette, appoint.

2. Definitions.—In this Act, [7]["the appropriate Government" means, in relation to Trade Unions whose objects are not confined to one State, the Central Government, and in relation to other Trade Unions, the State Government, and] unless there is anything repugnant in the subject or context,—

(*a*) "executive" means the body, by whatever name called, to which the management of the affairs of a Trade Union is entrusted;

(*b*) "[8][office-bearer]", in the case of a Trade Union, includes any member of the executive thereof, but does not include an auditor;

(*c*) "prescribed" means prescribed by regulations made under this Act;

(*d*) "registered office" means that office of a Trade Union which is registered under this Act as the head office thereof;

(*e*) "registered Trade Union" means a Trade Union registered under this Act;

[9][(*f*) "Registrar" means—

(*i*) a Registrar of Trade Unions appointed by the appropriate Government under section 3, and includes any Additional or Deputy Registrar of Trade Unions; and

(*ii*) in relation to any Trade Union, the Registrar appointed for the State in which

Figure: First Page of the Trade Unions Act 1946

7.1 Introduction and history of trade unions in India

Trade unions are organized groups of workers who collectively bargain for better pay, improved working conditions, and other labour rights. Historically, trade unions have played a crucial role in achieving labour reforms, such as the eight-hour workday and minimum wage standards.

Global Context

Trade unions emerged during the 19th century with the industrial revolution, particularly in Britain, where organized labour first gained prominence.

Indian Context

In India, the first trade union, the Bombay Mill-Hands Association, was founded by N.M. Lokhande in 1890. However, widespread unionization gained momentum after World War I, fueled by industrial growth and global labour movements like the Russian Revolution.

Key milestones include:

- **1918**: Establishment of the Madras Labour Union, the first registered union in India.

- **1920**: Formation of the All India Trade Union Congress (AITUC).

- **1926**: Enactment of the Trade Unions Act to regulate union activities.

Today, major national unions such as CITU, AITUC, INTUC, and the Bharatiya Mazdoor Sangh continue to represent workers across sectors. However, union membership has declined in newer industries like IT due to perceived professional status and higher salaries compared to traditional industries.

Figure: Logos of some of the trade unions in India.

7.2 Key Provisions of the Trade Unions Act

The Act provides a framework for the registration and regulation of trade unions. Key provisions include:

Registration

A trade union must be registered with a government-appointed registrar. The application should include:

- Names of office bearers.

- Rules of the trade union.

- Address of the registered office.

- Statement of assets and liabilities.

A minimum of 10% of the establishment's workforce or 100 workers, whichever is lower, must support the union's formation, with at least seven active members employed at the time of registration.

Rules of the Trade Union

The union's rules must define its objectives, permissible uses of funds, procedures for membership, amendments, audits, and dissolution. Funds can be used for members' welfare, legal expenses, and political affiliations.

Rights and Liabilities

Registered trade unions are legal entities, entitled to collective bargaining and representation in disputes. However, they must adhere to their registered rules and provide annual returns to the registrar.

Penalties

Unions failing to submit returns or providing false information may face penalties, including fines.

FORM A

Application for Registration of Trade Union

Dated the ....day of ....19..............

1- We hereby apply for the registration of a Trade Union under the name of

2- The Address of the head office of the Union is

3- The Union came in the existence on the ....day of ....19.....

4- The Union is a Union of employers (Workers engaged in the industry of profession).

5- The particulars required by section 5 (1) (c) of the Indian Trade Union Act. 1926.

6- The Particulars given in Schedule II show the provision made in the rules for the matters detailed in section 6 of the Indian Trade Union Act, 1926.

7- (To be struck out in the case of unions which have not been in existence for one year before the date of application. The particular required by section 5 (2) of the Indian Trade Union Act, 1926, are given in Schedule III.*

8. We have been duly authorized to make this application.

	Signature	Occupation	Address
Signed	1		
	2		
	3		
	4		
	5		
	6		
	7		

To the Registrar of Central Trade Unions , Delhi

* *State here whether the authority was given by a resolution of a general meeting of the Union, if not. in what other way it was given.*

Figure: Sample application for the registration of a trade union. This is accompanied with a list of officers, rules and statement of assets and liabilities of the trade union and a few other documents.

7.3 Decline of Trade Unions in New Industries

With the rise of the IT sector and other modern industries, trade union membership has waned. Workers in these sectors often perceive themselves as professionals rather than labourers, creating a cultural barrier to unionization. However, growing issues such as job insecurity and layoffs have led to the emergence of new unions in IT, such as the **Karnataka IT/ITES Union (KITU), AITES** and **Forum for IT Employees (FITE)**.

7.4 Conclusion

The Trade Unions Act has been a cornerstone of labour rights in India, enabling workers to organize and fight for fair treatment. While traditional industries continue to benefit from unionization, adapting the Act's principles to address the needs of new-age industries like IT could ensure broader protection for all workers.

Chapter 8: Code of Wages 2019

In this chapter we discuss the Code of Wages 2019, which is one of the four codes (Labour Codes) brought by the Indian government to simplify the labour laws in India. This code mainly deals with laws related to wages and salaries, overtime, bonus and minimum wages etc.

Figure: First page of the Code of Wages 2019

8.1 Introduction to the Code of Wages

The Code of Wages was enacted to unify and modernize wage-related laws in India. It replaces several earlier laws, including:

- Payment of Wages Act, 1936

- Minimum Wages Act, 1948

- Payment of Bonus Act, 1965

- Equal Remuneration Act, 1976

By consolidating these laws, the Code aims to:

- Ensure timely payment of wages.

- Mandate minimum wages across all sectors.

- Promote gender equality in remuneration.

8.2 Summary of the code of wages

Definition of Wages

The Code defines wages as the sum of basic pay, dearness allowance, and retention allowance. It excludes bonuses, employer-provided accommodation, contributions to provident funds, and gratuity. The excluded components must not exceed 50% of the total wages.

Minimum Wages

A national floor wage is determined by the central government, considering the cost of living.

State governments cannot set minimum wages below the national floor wage.

Wages are classified based on skill levels and work nature and must be reviewed every five years.

Payment of Wages

Employers can pay wages in cash, by cheque, or electronically.

Deductions are allowed only for specified reasons, such as fines or recovery of advances, and must not exceed 50% of the total wages.

Working Hours and Overtime

A standard workday is set at 8 hours, with a mandatory rest day every seven days.

Overtime must be compensated at twice the regular wage rate.

Bonus Entitlement

Employees earning below a certain threshold and who have worked at least 30 days in a year are entitled to a bonus.

Bonuses range between 8.33% and 20% of annual wages and are derived from the company's surplus profits.

Gender Equality

The Code prohibits wage discrimination based on gender for similar work.

It encourages the participation of women in the workforce through advisory boards.

Grievance Redressal

Authorities are appointed to handle disputes related to wage payments, with the aim of resolving cases within three months.

Penalties for Violations

Employers who fail to comply with the Code can face imprisonment of up to three months and fines of up to ₹1 lakh.

8.3 Practical Implications

The Code has streamlined wage-related regulations, making it easier for employers to comply while ensuring workers' rights.

It provides clarity on wage structures and ensures a fair minimum wage across all sectors.

The provisions for gender equality and timely payment address long-standing issues in labour practices.

Digital record-keeping and web-based inspections improve transparency and accountability.

8.4 Conclusion

The Code of Wages, 2019 is a comprehensive reform aimed at creating a uniform framework for wage regulation in India. Its emphasis on fair pay, gender equality, and improved enforcement mechanisms marks a significant step toward enhancing labour welfare.

Chapter 9: Occupational Safety, Health and Working Conditions Code 2020

In this chapter, we discuss the Occupational Safety, Health, and Working Conditions Code, 2020 (OHS Code), a significant reform introduced to consolidate and modernize laws related to workplace safety and employee welfare.

9.1 Introduction to the OHS Code

The OHS Code aims to ensure safe and healthy working conditions across various industries in India. It consolidates 13 existing laws, including:

- Contract Labour (Regulation and Abolition) Act, 1970

- Factories Act, 1948

- Mines Act, 1952

- Inter-State Migrant Workers Act, 1979

The Code applies to establishments employing 20 or more workers in factories using power and 40 or more workers in those without power.

सी.जी.-डी.एल.-अ.-29092020-222112
CG-DL-E-29092020-222112

असाधारण
EXTRAORDINARY

भाग II — खण्ड 1
PART II — Section 1

प्राधिकार से प्रकाशित
PUBLISHED BY AUTHORITY

सं० 62]   नई दिल्ली, मंगलवार, सितम्बर 29, 2020/ आश्विन 7, 1942 (शक)
No. 62]   NEW DELHI, TUESDAY, SEPTEMBER 29, 2020/ASVINA 7, 1942 (SAKA)

इस भाग में भिन्न पृष्ठ संख्या दी जाती है जिससे कि यह अलग संकलन के रूप में रखा जा सके।
Separate paging is given to this Part in order that it may be filed as a separate compilation.

MINISTRY OF LAW AND JUSTICE
(Legislative Department)

New Delhi, the 29th September, 2020/Asvina 7, 1942 (Saka)

The following Act of Parliament received the assent of the President on the 28th September, 2020 and is hereby published for general information:—

THE OCCUPATIONAL SAFETY, HEALTH AND WORKING CONDITIONS CODE, 2020

No. 37 of 2020

[28th September, 2020.]

An Act to consolidate and amend the laws regulating the occupational safety, health and working conditions of the persons employed in an establishment and for matters connected therewith or incidental thereto.

Be it enacted by Parliament in the Seventy-first Year of the Republic of India as follows:—

CHAPTER I
PRELIMINARY

1. (*1*) This Act may be called the Occupational Safety, Health and Working Conditions Code, 2020.

(*2*) It shall come into force on such date as the Central Government may, by notification appoint; and different dates may be appointed for different provisions of this Code and any reference in any such provision to the commencement of this Code shall be construed as a reference to the coming into force of that provision.

Short title, commencement and application.

Figure: First page of the OHS Code 2020

9.2 Key Provisions of the OHS code

Working Hours and Leave

The maximum daily work duration is set at 8 hours, with a six-day workweek.

Workers are entitled to annual leave and leave encashment benefits.

Contract Labour and Inter-State Migrant Workers

Contract labour provisions include clear responsibilities for contractors and principal employers.

Inter-state migrant workers are entitled to fair wages, travel allowances, and insurance coverage.

Provisions for Women Workers

Women can be employed in night shifts (7 PM to 6 AM) with their consent, provided adequate safety measures are in place.

Health and Safety Measures

The Code mandates the following workplace facilities:

- Separate washing, bathing, and locker facilities for male and female employees.

- Provision of clean drinking water, first aid, adequate lighting, and ventilation.

- Creche facilities for establishments with a certain number of female employees.

National and State-Level Advisory Boards

The Code establishes a National Occupational Safety and Health Advisory Board and similar state-level boards to oversee implementation and recommend policy changes.

Simplification of Procedures

A single license and unified electronic registration system replace multiple registrations under earlier laws.

Employers are required to submit one consolidated annual return instead of separate filings.

9.3 Impact on Employers and Employees

The OHS Code benefits employers by streamlining compliance procedures and reducing regulatory burdens. For employees, it enhances safety standards, ensures access to basic amenities, and provides clear guidelines for grievance redressal.

9.4 Conclusion

The Occupational Safety, Health, and Working Conditions Code, 2020, represents a comprehensive effort to enhance workplace safety and welfare. By consolidating existing laws and introducing modern measures, it ensures better working conditions while balancing the needs of employers and employees.

Chapter 10: Code on Social Security 2020

In this chapter we discuss the Code on Social Security 2020, which is one of the four new codes brought by the Indian government to reform and simplify the labour laws. It consolidates the laws related to the social security benefits for all employees in the organized and unorganized sectors.

सी.जी.-डी.एल.-अ.-29092020-222111
CG-DL-E-29092020-222111

असाधारण
EXTRAORDINARY

भाग II — खण्ड 1
PART II — Section 1

प्राधिकार से प्रकाशित
PUBLISHED BY AUTHORITY

सं. 61] नई दिल्ली, मंगलवार, सितम्बर 29, 2020/ आश्विन 7, 1942 (शक)
No. 61] NEW DELHI, TUESDAY, SEPTEMBER 29, 2020/ASVINA 7, 1942 (SAKA) .

इस भाग में भिन्न पृष्ठ संख्या दी जाती है जिससे कि यह अलग संकलन के रूप में रखा जा सके।
Separate paging is given to this Part in order that it may be filed as a separate compilation.

MINISTRY OF LAW AND JUSTICE
(Legislative Department)

New Delhi, the 29th September, 2020/Asvina 7, 1942 (Saka)

The following Act of Parliament received the assent of the President on the 28th September, 2020 and is hereby published for general information:—

THE CODE ON SOCIAL SECURITY, 2020

No. 36 of 2020

[*28th September, 2020.*]

An Act to amend and consolidate the laws relating to social security with the goal to extend social security to all employees and workers either in the organised or unorganised or any other sectors and for matters connected therewith or incidental thereto.

BE it enacted by Parliament in the Seventy-first Year of the Republic of India as follows:—

CHAPTER I
PRELIMINARY

1. (*1*) This Act may be called the Code on Social Security, 2020.

(*2*) It extends to the whole of India.

(*3*) It shall come into force on such date as the Central Government may, by notification in the Official Gazette, appoint; and different dates may be appointed for different provisions of this Code and any reference in any such provision to the commencement of this Code shall be construed as a reference to the coming into force of that provision.

Short title, extent, commencement and application

Figure: First page of the Code on Social Security 2020

10.1 Introduction to the code on Social Security

The Code on Social Security was enacted to consolidate and simplify existing laws related to social security and employee welfare. It replaces several older acts, including:

- Employees' Compensation Act, 1923

- Employees' State Insurance Act, 1948

- Employees' Provident Funds and Miscellaneous Provisions Act, 1952

- Maternity Benefit Act, 1961

- Payment of Gratuity Act, 1972

- Unorganised Workers' Social Security Act, 2008

The Code broadens the scope of social security by including gig workers, platform workers, and unorganized sector employees, in addition to those in formal employment.

10.2 Key Provisions of the code on social security

Social Security Coverage

The Code mandates benefits such as life insurance, disability insurance, maternity benefits, provident fund, pension, and gratuity for all eligible workers, including gig and platform workers.

Employees' Provident Fund (EPF)

EPF provisions apply to establishments employing 20 or more workers.

Employers must contribute 10% of employees' wages to the fund, matched by employee contributions.

Employees' State Insurance (ESI)

ESI applies to establishments with 10 or more employees and includes provisions for hazardous occupations with even a single employee.

Workers are insured for medical treatment, maternity, disability, and other benefits.

Gratuity Entitlement

Gratuity is extended to fixed-term employees in addition to permanent employees.

It is payable in cases of resignation, retirement, or death, regardless of the length of service for fixed-term workers.

Maternity Benefits

The Code includes comprehensive maternity benefits, ensuring paid leave and job security for women during pregnancy and postpartum recovery.

Gig and Platform Workers

For the first time, gig and platform workers are eligible for social security benefits, including health insurance, accident insurance, and retirement benefits.

Unified Administration

The Code introduces a central and state-level Social Security Board to oversee the implementation of benefits.

It mandates electronic record-keeping and compliance, reducing administrative burdens for employers.

Penalties for Non-Compliance

Employers who fail to comply with the Code may face fines or imprisonment, ensuring accountability and enforcement.

10.3 Implications for Employers and Employees

The Code simplifies compliance by unifying multiple social security regulations under a single framework. For employees, especially those in unorganized and gig sectors, it provides a safety net that was previously unavailable.

10.4 Conclusion

The Code on Social Security, 2020, marks a significant step in ensuring comprehensive and equitable social security for all workers in India. Its inclusive provisions and streamlined processes aim to improve the well-being of workers while balancing the needs of employers.

Chapter 11: Industrial Relations Code 2020

In this chapter we discuss the Industrial Relations Code 2020, which is one of the four new codes brought by the Indian government to reform and simplify the labour laws. It reforms existing laws related to trade unions, conditions of employment and industrial disputes.

MINISTRY OF LAW AND JUSTICE
(Legislative Department)

New Delhi, the 29th September, 2020/Asvina 7, 1942 (Saka)

The following Act of Parliament received the assent of the President on the 28th September, 2020 and is hereby published for general information:—

THE INDUSTRIAL RELATIONS CODE, 2020

No. 35 of 2020

[*28th September, 2020.*]

An Act to consolidate and amend the laws relating to Trade Unions, conditions of employment in industrial establishment or undertaking, investigation and settlement of industrial disputes and for matters connected therewith or incidental thereto.

Be it enacted by Parliament in the Seventy-first Year of the Republic of India as follows:—

CHAPTER I

Preliminary

1. (*1*) This Act may be called the Industrial Relations Code, 2020.

(*2*) It shall extend to the whole of India.

(*3*) It shall come into force on such date as the Central Government may, by notification in the Official Gazette appoint; and different dates may be appointed for different provisions of this Code and any reference in any such provision to the commencement of this Code shall be construed as a reference to the coming into force of that provision.

Figure: First page of the Industrial Relations Code 2020

11.1 Introduction to the Industrial Relations Code

The Industrial Relations Code was introduced to reform existing laws and provide a unified framework for managing employer-employee relationships. It replaces three major laws:

- Trade Unions Act 1926

- Industrial Employment (Standing Orders) Act 1946

- Industrial Disputes Act 1947

The Code aims to balance the flexibility needs of employers with the rights and protections of workers.

11.2 Key Provisions of the Industrial Relations Code 2020

The industrial relations code introduces more conditions for a legal strike by workers and increases the threshold for layoffs and firings without getting government permission to 300 workers from the existing 100. It thus focuses on providing more flexibility to employers to hire and fire workers.

It provides a broader framework for workers to form unions. It introduces new concepts for recognition of trade unions as follows: if there is only a single union in a company it is recognized as the sole trade union. In case of multiple unions, the one with 51% workers is recognized. If no union has 51% workers, the employer forms a negotiating council with representatives of the registered trade unions.

It amends the definition of strike to mass casual leave. If 50% or more employees go on casual leave, then it is treated as a strike. However workers cannot go on a strike without 14 days notice. No employer can lock out any employees without at least 14 days notice. Lockouts and strikes are prohibited after 7 days of arbitration, or during the period of an arbitration award or settlement award. The government has the power to postpone enforcement of the tribunal awards.

Complaint redressal committees are required for establishments with more than 20 employees, with not exceeding 10 members and equal representation from the employees and management side.

Standing orders are required for establishments with 300 or more employees.

The code provides for a reskilling fund for laid off employees, which is used to pay the last 15 days salary for the laid off worker within 45 days of the dismissal. 50% of the basic wages and dearness allowance should be paid if an employee is laid off. In case of retrenchment, one months' notice or equivalent salary must be given and 15 days salary for each year of continuous service completed must be paid.

11.3 Implications of the Code

For Employers: The Code provides greater flexibility in hiring and firing, simplifying compliance requirements for larger organizations.

For Employees: It offers protections against unfair practices, ensures timely resolution of disputes, and provides financial support through the reskilling fund.

11.4 Conclusion

The Industrial Relations Code, 2020, aims to foster harmonious industrial relations by streamlining laws and addressing both employer and employee needs. While its provisions enhance flexibility for employers, the focus on grievance redressal and worker protections ensures a balanced approach.

Chapter 12: Remedies for Unfair Dismissal from a Job

In this chapter, we explore the actions an employee can take when faced with unfair dismissal or retrenchment, along with the legal remedies available under Indian labour laws.

12.1 Unfair Dismissal

Unfair dismissal or termination of employment is where an employer terminates the employment of an employee without giving a strong and valid reason.

As per the **Industrial Relations Code 2020**, termination of employment for any reason other than disciplinary action comes under retrenchment. This requires a month's written notice period on part of the employer, along with 15 days of average pay as compensation for every year of active service with that employer.

Some employers, to avoid paying the compensation and other legal steps, try to force the employees to resign. However, forced resignation is not valid or legal as per the labour laws in India.

12.2 Retrenchments in the Industrial Relations Code 2020

The code states the following provisions related to layoffs and retrenchments:

"retrenchment" means the termination by the employer of the service of a worker for any reason whatsoever, otherwise than as a punishment inflicted by way of disciplinary action,

No worker employed in any industry who has been in continuous service for not less than one year under an employer shall be retrenched by that employer until—

(a) the worker has been given one month's notice in writing indicating the reasons for retrenchment and the period of notice has expired, or the worker has been paid in lieu of such notice, wages for the period of the notice;

(b) the worker has been paid, at the time of retrenchment, compensation which shall be equivalent to fifteen days' average pay, or average pay of such days as may be notified by the appropriate Government, for every completed year of continuous service or any part thereof in excess of six months; and

(c) notice in such manner as may be prescribed is served on the appropriate Government or such authority as may be specified by the appropriate Government by notification.

67. Whenever a worker (other than a badli worker or a casual worker) whose name is borne on the muster rolls of an industrial establishment and who has completed not less than one year of continuous service under an employer is laid-off, whether continuously or intermittently, he shall be paid by the employer for all days during which he is so laid-off, except for such weekly holidays as may intervene, compensation which shall be equal to fifty per cent. of the total of the basic wages and dearness allowance that would have been payable to him, had he not been so laid-off:

Provided that if during any period of twelve months, a worker is so laid-off for more than forty-five days, no such compensation shall be payable in respect of any period of the lay-off after the expiry of the first forty-five days, if there is an agreement to that effect between the worker and the employer:

Provided further that it shall be lawful for the employer in any case falling within the foregoing proviso to retrench the worker in accordance with the provisions contained in section 70 at any time after the expiry of the first forty-five days of the lay-off and when he does so, any compensation paid to the worker for having been laid-off during the preceding twelve months may be set off against the compensation payable for retrenchment.

12.3 Remedies in case of unfair dismissal

Approaching Labour Authorities

Employees can file a complaint with the labour commissioner or labour boards. These authorities facilitate conciliation between the employee and employer to resolve disputes.

Legal Action

If conciliation fails, employees can approach the industrial tribunal or labour court. Under Indian labour laws, courts have the power to:

- Reinstate the employee.

- Award compensation for wrongful dismissal.

Union Support

Employees can seek assistance from trade unions for legal representation and negotiation with employers. Established unions like CITU, AITUC, and INTUC often provide legal and strategic support.

Anti-Discrimination Claims

If dismissal involves discrimination—such as gender-based wage disparity—employees can file separate claims under applicable laws like the Code of Wages, 2019 or the Sexual Harassment of Women at Workplace Act, 2013.

Documentation

Employees should maintain records of communication with employers, including emails and meeting notes, to substantiate claims in case of legal action.

12.4 Key Considerations for Employees

Forced resignations are illegal and can be challenged.

Employees should be aware of their rights under the Industrial Disputes Act, 1947, and the Industrial Relations Code, 2020.

Blacklisting by employers as retaliation is also unlawful and can be contested in court.

12.5 Conclusion

Unfair dismissal remains a pressing issue in the Indian workforce. By understanding their rights and leveraging available legal remedies, employees can challenge wrongful practices and secure fair treatment. Awareness of labour laws and support from unions or legal advisors can make a significant difference in such cases.

Chapter 13: Laws Related to Sexual Harassment at Work

In this chapter we discuss the laws related to sexual harassment at work. Since sexual harassment at work is a major issue especially for the well-being of female employees and creating a hostile work environment, it has been dealt with in the labour laws.

THE SEXUAL HARASSMENT OF WOMEN AT WORKPLACE
(PREVENTION, PROHIBITION AND REDRESSAL) ACT, 2013

ACT NO. 14 OF 2013

[22nd April, 2013]

An Act to provide protection against sexual harassment of women at workplace and for the prevention and redressal of complaints of sexual harassment and for matters connected therewith or incidental thereto.

WHEREAS sexual harassment results in violation of the fundamental rights of a woman to equality under articles 14 and 15 of the Constitution of India and her right to life and to live with dignity under article 21 of the Constitution and right to practice any profession or to carry on any occupation, trade or business with includes a right to a safe environment free from sexual harassment;

AND WHEREAS the protection against sexual harassment and the right to work with dignity are universally recognised human rights by international conventions and instruments such as Convention on the Elimination of all Forms of Discrimination against Women, which has been ratified on the 25th June, 1993 by the Government of India;

AND WHEREAS it is expedient to make provisions for giving effect to the said Convention for protection of women against sexual harassment at workplace.

BE it enacted by Parliament in the Sixty-fourth Year of the Republic of India as follows: —

CHAPTER I

PRELIMINARY

1. Short title, extent and commencement.—(*1*) This Act may be called the Sexual Harassment of Women at Workplace (Prevention, Prohibition and Redressal) Act, 2013.

(*2*) It extends to the whole of India.

(*3*) It shall come into force on such date¹ as the Central Government may, by notification in the Official Gazette, appoint.

2. Definitions.—In this Act, unless the context otherwise requires, —

(*a*) "aggrieved woman" means—

(*i*) in relation to a workplace, a woman, of any age whether employed or not, who alleges to have been subjected to any act of sexual harassment by the respondent;

(*ii*) in relation to dwelling place or house, a woman of any age who is employed in such a dwelling place or house;

(*b*) "appropriate Government" means—

(*i*) in relation to a workplace which is established, owned, controlled or wholly or substantially financed by funds provided directly or indirectly—

(*A*) by the Central Government or the Union territory administration, the Central Government;

Figure: First page of the Sexual Harassment Act 2013

13.1 Introduction to the Sexual Harassment of Women at Workplace Act

The Sexual Harassment of Women at Workplace (Prevention, Prohibition and Redressal) Act was passed in 2013 by the government. It provides for an environment which ensures the women's right to workplace equality and freedom from sexual harassment.

13.2 Summary of the Sexual Harassment Act

Sexual harassment includes unwanted and unwelcome acts towards women including physical contact and advances, demands or requests for sexual favours, making sexually coloured remarks, showing pornography or any other unwelcome physical, verbal or non-verbal conduct of sexual nature.

If a women employee is promised preferential treatment or threatened with detrimental treatment conditional on the giving of sexual favours, it constitutes sexual harassment.

The company shall constitute an internal complaints committee, consisting of a woman presiding officer from the management and one or two male or female employees, for investigation of complaints. It may also file a local committee.

Any woman may approach the committee with her complaint with details in writing within three months of the incident. The committee may on the request of the woman attempt to settle the dispute through conciliation, failing which they will proceed with their inquiry. The committee can forward the complaint to the police if it deems fit, such as if the woman states the respondent is not complying with the terms and conditions of the settlement.

The complaints committee shall have the same powers as are vested in a civil court in relation to summoning and examining witnesses under oath and examining evidence.

The remedies available are various types of relief including transfer of the victim or respondent to another workplace, granting of leave to the aggrieved women up to three months or other kinds of relief. They can also pay compensation for the loss and trauma as well as career opportunity loss and medical expenses, to the aggrieved woman. It may also restrain the respondent from reporting on the work performance of the aggrieved woman.

As per the law, the employer also has a responsibility for a harassment free and safe working environment at the workplace. To that end they may constitute Prevention of Sexual Harassment or POSH workshops or training programs for all employees, raise awareness of the internal committee, treat sexual harassment as misconduct under the service rules and report on the number of such cases filed and disposed. If the employer does not comply with the requirements, they can be punished including removal of their license to operate the business.

13.3 Conclusion

In this chapter we have discussed the Sexual Harassment of Women at Workplace (Prevention, Prohibition and Redressal) Act, 2013, which aims to make the workplace a safe and equitable environment for women. The Act places clear obligations on employers to establish internal redressal mechanisms and to foster a culture of zero tolerance toward harassment. For IT employees, particularly women working long hours or in remote and isolated settings, awareness of this law is an important step toward asserting their rights and seeking recourse when   needed.

Chapter 14: How to Form an IT Trade Union

In this chapter, we explore the steps and considerations involved in forming a trade union for IT workers in India. With increasing challenges such as layoffs, poor working conditions, and job insecurity, IT trade unions have become vital for safeguarding employee rights.

14.1 Why IT Employees Need Trade Unions

Historically, IT workers were perceived as professionals exempt from traditional labour issues due to their higher salaries and white-collar status. However, the rise in layoffs, exploitation, and increasing pressure from automation and globalization has highlighted the need for collective action.

Trade unions provide:

- A platform for collective bargaining.

- Legal and financial support during disputes.

- Advocacy for better working conditions and job security.

14.2 Steps to Form an IT Trade Union

Step 1: Understand Legal Requirements

Under the Trade Unions Act, 1926, a union must have:

- At least seven members from the same establishment or industry.

- A written constitution outlining the union's objectives and rules.

- Membership that represents at least 10% of the workforce or 100 workers, whichever is less.

Step 2: Draft a Constitution

The union's constitution should include:

- Objectives and purposes.

- Rules for membership eligibility and fees.

- Election procedures for office bearers.

- Provisions for financial management, audits, and annual returns.

Step 3: Elect Office Bearers

The union must appoint office bearers (e.g., president, secretary, treasurer) from among its members. At least 50% of office bearers must be employed in the establishment or industry.

Step 4: Register the Union

To register the union with the Registrar of Trade Unions, submit:

- The completed application form.

- The union's constitution.

- A list of office bearers and their details.

- A statement of assets and liabilities.

Upon approval, the union receives a certificate of registration, granting it legal recognition.

Step 5: Engage and Mobilize Members

Build awareness about the union's goals and benefits among employees. Encourage active participation to strengthen the union's influence and bargaining power.

14.3 Challenges in Forming IT Trade Unions

Employer Resistance: IT companies often discourage union activities, citing concerns over productivity and global competitiveness.

Legal and Procedural Barriers: Bureaucratic delays in registration can discourage unionization efforts.

Lack of Awareness: Many IT employees remain unaware of their rights or are hesitant to join unions due to fear of retaliation.

Cultural Stigma: The white-collar image of IT workers leads to misconceptions about the necessity of unions in the sector.

14.4 Success Stories of IT Trade Unions

Organizations like Karnataka IT/ITES Employees Union (KITU) and Forum for IT Employees (FITE) have successfully advocated for workers' rights, challenging unfair layoffs and promoting awareness of labour rights.

For example, FITE played a significant role in raising awareness about illegal terminations in major IT companies and provided legal support to affected employees.

14.5 Conclusion

Forming an IT trade union is a critical step toward addressing the challenges faced by employees in the Indian IT sector. While obstacles exist, unions provide an essential platform for collective action, enabling workers to negotiate for better working conditions and job security.

Chapter 15: Why IT Employees Need Trade Unions

In this chapter, we delve deeper into the necessity of trade unions for IT employees in India, addressing the unique challenges faced by this workforce and the benefits of collective action.

15.1 The Evolving Nature of IT Work

The Indian IT industry, once celebrated as a stable and lucrative career path, now faces increasing volatility. Automation, global competition, and cost-cutting measures have transformed the work environment, leading to:

- Frequent layoffs and forced resignations.

- Extended working hours without additional compensation.

- Stressful and exploitative work cultures.

- Lack of legal protections for gig and contract workers in IT.

These challenges have revealed the need for a collective voice to advocate for employee rights and fair practices.

15.2 Common Issues Faced by IT Employees

Job Insecurity

Periodic layoffs, often justified by cost-cutting measures or performance reviews, leave employees vulnerable. Mid-level employees, in particular, face challenges due to limited opportunities for reskilling.

Unfair Work Practices

- Overwork without overtime pay.

- Lack of transparency in performance evaluations.

- Pressures to resign under threat of poor appraisals or blacklisting.

Health and Well-Being

Chronic health issues like repetitive strain injuries (RSI) and stress-related disorders.

Poor work-life balance due to demanding schedules.

Lack of Legal Awareness

Many IT workers are unaware of their rights under labour laws, making them more susceptible to exploitation.

Resistance to Unionization

Employers often discourage union formation, emphasizing the industry's professional status and claiming unions would disrupt productivity.

15.3 Benefits of Trade Unions for IT Employees

Collective Bargaining

Unions negotiate for better wages, improved working conditions, and job security on behalf of employees.

Legal Support

They provide guidance and representation in cases of unfair dismissal, harassment, or disputes over compensation.

Awareness and Advocacy

Unions educate employees about their rights and work to address broader industry issues, such as excessive work hours and gender inequality.

Emotional Support

In high-stress environments, unions offer solidarity and a sense of community, reducing isolation and burnout.

Influencing Policy

Through organized action, unions can advocate for stronger labour laws and policies that protect IT workers.

15.4 Examples of IT Trade Unions in Action

Karnataka IT/ITES Employees Union (KITU): KITU has successfully challenged unfair layoffs and provided legal aid to affected employees in Karnataka's IT sector.

Forum for IT Employees (FITE): FITE has been instrumental in raising awareness about workers' rights and supporting employees during mass layoffs in companies like Cognizant and Tech Mahindra.

15.5 Conclusion

The IT industry, despite its professional status, is not immune to labour issues. Trade unions provide a critical platform for addressing these challenges, ensuring fair treatment and protection for employees. By fostering collective action, unions empower IT workers to demand better working conditions and contribute to a more equitable industry.

Chapter 16: Legal Protections for IT Employees in India

In this chapter, we explore the various labour laws and legal protections available to IT employees in India. While the IT sector has historically been exempt from certain traditional labour laws, recent developments have introduced frameworks to address employee rights in this industry.

16.1 Applicability of Labour Laws to IT Employees

The Indian IT sector was initially exempt from certain labour regulations under the guise of maintaining flexibility and global competitiveness. However, with increasing concerns about layoffs, workplace stress, and unfair practices, labour protections are being extended to IT workers.

Key laws applicable to IT employees include:

Industrial Disputes Act, 1947: Governs layoffs, retrenchments, and dispute resolution mechanisms.

Shops and Establishments Act (State-specific): Regulates working hours, leave policies, and working conditions in commercial establishments, including IT firms.

Maternity Benefit Act, 1961: Provides paid maternity leave and job security for women employees.

Code on Wages, 2019: Ensures minimum wages and prohibits gender-based wage discrimination.

Sexual Harassment of Women at Workplace (Prevention, Prohibition, and Redressal) Act, 2013: Mandates the establishment of Internal Complaints Committees (ICCs) to address workplace harassment.

16.2 Protections Against Unfair Termination

Under the Industrial Disputes Act, 1947 and the Industrial Relations Code, 2020, IT employees are entitled to:

Notice Period: One month's written notice or equivalent pay.

Severance Pay: Compensation of 15 days' wages for every completed year of service in cases of retrenchment.

Protection from Forced Resignation: Employers cannot coerce employees into resigning to avoid retrenchment obligations.

16.3 Regulations on Working Hours and Leave

The Shops and Establishments Act mandates:

- A maximum of 48 working hours per week.

- Overtime pay for work beyond the stipulated hours.

- One mandatory day off every week.

- Annual leave, sick leave, and casual leave entitlements vary by state, but employers must comply with the respective state laws.

16.4 Addressing Workplace Harassment

The Sexual Harassment of Women at Workplace Act, 2013 ensures:

- Establishment of ICCs in companies with 10 or more employees.

- Strict timelines for resolving complaints.

- Confidentiality for complainants.

16.5 Enforcement Mechanisms

Employees can seek recourse through:

Labour Commissioners: They mediate disputes and ensure compliance with labour laws.

Industrial Tribunals: These adjudicate cases related to layoffs, unfair dismissals, and other labour disputes.

Internal Committees: For workplace harassment, employees can approach the company's ICC.

16.6 Challenges in Enforcing Rights

While laws exist, their implementation often falls short due to:

- Limited awareness among employees about their rights.

- Delays in legal processes, deterring employees from pursuing cases.

- Employer resistance to unionization or grievances.

16.7 Conclusion

Legal protections for IT employees in India have improved significantly over the years, but enforcement remains a challenge. Greater awareness and robust implementation are essential to ensure that IT employees can benefit fully from these protections and work in fair and supportive environments.

Chapter 17: Conclusion

In this book, we have discussed some issues with the IT sector in India. We have gone through the topic of retrenchments or involuntary terminations of IT employees, often without following the applicable labour laws of India.

In this chapter, we summarize the key remedies and protections available to IT employees in India, ensuring they understand their rights and the steps to address common workplace challenges.

17.1 Understanding the Landscape

The IT sector, while offering lucrative opportunities, also exposes employees to unique challenges such as layoffs, unfair dismissal, and overwork. Being informed about available remedies is the first step toward addressing these issues effectively.

17.2 Remedies for Layoffs and Retrenchment

Legal Protections Under the Industrial Relations Code, 2020:

Employers must provide one month's notice or equivalent pay before retrenching an employee.

Severance pay equivalent to 15 days' wages for every year of service is mandatory.

Filing Complaints

Employees can file a complaint with the labour commissioner if retrenchment conditions are not met.

Industrial tribunals can be approached for dispute resolution.

Union Support

Trade unions like KITU and FITE provide legal and strategic assistance during mass layoffs.

17.3 Remedies for Unfair Dismissal

Forced Resignations

Employees pressured into resigning can contest the validity of their resignation in court.

Maintaining documentation of all communication with HR and management is crucial.

Legal Action

Approach industrial tribunals or courts for compensation or reinstatement.

Support from Trade Unions

Engage with unions for guidance and collective action.

17.4 Addressing Workplace Harassment

Internal Complaints Committees (ICCs)

Employees can file complaints with their company's ICC under the Sexual Harassment of Women at Workplace Act, 2013.

ICCs are obligated to resolve complaints within a specified timeframe while maintaining confidentiality.

Legal Recourse

If ICCs fail to act, employees can escalate the matter to local labour authorities or courts.

17.5 Remedies for Overwork and Poor Working Conditions

State Shops and Establishments Act

Ensures regulated working hours and mandatory weekly time off.

Employees can approach labour commissioners to report violations.

Employee Grievance Committees

Companies with more than 20 employees must establish grievance committees to address complaints about working conditions.

17.6 Protecting Gig and Contract Workers

Social Security Provisions

The Code on Social Security, 2020, extends benefits such as insurance and retirement savings to gig and platform workers.

Legal Advocacy

Non-unionized workers can approach labour welfare boards established under the new labour codes.

17.7 Building Awareness

Employees should familiarize themselves with applicable labour laws, including the Industrial Relations Code, Code on Wages, and Occupational Safety, Health, and Working Conditions Code.

Seeking guidance from trade unions, legal experts, or labour consultants can provide additional support.

17.8 Conclusion

The Indian IT sector has grown rapidly, but with growth come challenges that require employees to be proactive in understanding and asserting their rights. By leveraging the remedies and protections summarized in this chapter, IT employees can address workplace challenges and ensure fair treatment.

Glossary of Key Terms

This glossary defines key legal and industry terms used throughout the book, intended as a quick reference for readers unfamiliar with Indian labour law terminology.

Bell Curve System: A performance appraisal method in which employees are ranked on a distribution curve, with a fixed percentage designated as low performers regardless of absolute performance. Widely used in Indian IT companies as a cost-cutting mechanism.

BPO (Business Process Outsourcing): The practice of contracting specific business operations or functions to a third-party service provider. India is a global hub for BPO services, particularly in customer support, data entry, and back-office operations.

Collective Bargaining: A process of negotiation between an employer and a group of employees, typically represented by a trade union, aimed at reaching an agreement on wages, working hours, and other conditions of employment.

Contract Labour: Workers hired through a third-party contractor rather than directly by the company where they work. Contract labourers typically have fewer legal protections and benefits than permanent employees.

EPF (Employees' Provident Fund): A government-mandated retirement savings scheme in India where both the employer and employee contribute a percentage of the employee's wages each month. The accumulated fund is accessible to the employee upon retirement, resignation, or in cases of emergency.

ESI (Employees' State Insurance): A social insurance scheme providing medical, sickness, maternity, disability, and death benefits to eligible employees and their dependents. Administered by the Employees' State Insurance Corporation (ESIC).

Forced Resignation: A situation where an employer pressures, coerces, or threatens an employee to resign voluntarily in order to avoid the legal obligations associated with formal retrenchment. Forced resignation is illegal under Indian labour law and can be challenged in court.

Gig Worker: A worker engaged in short-term, flexible, or project-based work, typically through a digital platform (such as a ride-hailing or food delivery app). Gig workers are now partially covered under the Code on Social Security, 2020.

Gratuity: A lump-sum payment made by an employer to an employee as a token of gratitude for services rendered. Under Indian law, gratuity is payable to employees who have completed five or more years of continuous service upon resignation, retirement, or death.

ICC (Internal Complaints Committee): A committee mandated by the Sexual Harassment of Women at Workplace Act, 2013, to be constituted by every employer with 10 or more employees. The ICC investigates complaints of sexual harassment and recommends appropriate action.

Industrial Dispute: A dispute or difference between employers and employees, or between employees and employees, connected with the employment, non-employment, or terms of service of any person. Industrial disputes are governed by the Industrial Disputes Act, 1947, and subsequently by the Industrial Relations Code, 2020.

NASSCOM: The National Association of Software and Service Companies, India's apex trade body for the IT-BPM (Information Technology – Business Process Management) sector. NASSCOM represents approximately 3,000 member companies and plays a significant role in policy advocacy for the industry.

Retrenchment: The termination of employment by an employer for any reason other than disciplinary action. Under the Industrial Relations Code, 2020, employees with at least one year of continuous service are entitled to one month's notice and severance pay equivalent to 15 days' wages for each completed year of service.

RSI (Repetitive Strain Injury): A group of musculoskeletal conditions caused by repetitive tasks, forceful exertions, vibrations, or sustained awkward positions. Common among IT professionals who spend long hours at computers, RSI can affect the wrists, hands, forearms, shoulders, and neck.

SEZ (Special Economic Zone): A geographically defined area within a country that operates under distinct economic regulations intended to attract foreign investment and promote exports. In India, SEZs offer tax holidays and reduced regulatory burdens, including partial exemptions from standard labour laws.

Standing Orders: Written rules that define the terms and conditions of employment in an establishment, including working hours, disciplinary procedures, leave entitlements, and grounds for dismissal. Required under the Industrial Employment (Standing Orders) Act, 1946, for establishments above a specified size.

Trade Union: An organized association of workers formed to protect and promote their collective interests, including wages, working conditions, and job security. Trade unions are regulated in India by the Trade Unions Act, 1926, and the Industrial Relations Code, 2020.

Unfair Labour Practice: Actions by an employer or trade union that violate the rights of employees or employers as defined by labour law. Examples include interfering with the right to form a union, threatening employees for union activities, or forming a management-controlled "dummy" union. These are prohibited under the Industrial Relations Code, 2020.

About the authors

Siva Prasad Bose is a retired electrical engineer and writer of introductory guides on aspects of law in India. He is retired after many years of service in Uttar Pradesh Power Corporation Limited (UPPCL, formerly UPSEB). He received his engineering degree from Jadavpur University, Kolkata and has a law degree from Meerut University, Meerut and a BSc from MMH College Ghaziabad. His interests lie in the fields of family law, civil law, law of contracts, and any areas of law related to electric power related issues.

Joy Bose is a data scientist by profession, with experience working in the technology industry in India and internationally. He has a keen interest in the intersection of technology, labour rights, and public policy.

Other books by Siva Prasad Bose

Introduction to Wills and Probate

Senior Citizens Abuse in India: And what to do about it

Introduction to Negotiable Instruments: As per Indian laws

Introduction to Marriage Laws in India

Managing Court Cases with Mental Strength

Self-Publish Books and E-Books in India

Delays in Court Cases in India

Introduction to Patents and Patent Law in India

Introduction to Property Law in India

Introduction to Tort Law in India